# Track and Field

**BY MATT DOEDEN**

AMICUS HIGH INTEREST ❦ AMICUS INK

Amicus High Interest and Amicus Ink are imprints of Amicus
P.O. Box 1329, Mankato, MN 56002
www.amicuspublishing.us

Library of Congress Cataloging-in-Publication Data
Doeden, Matt.
 Track and field / Matt Doeden.
    pages cm. – (Summer Olympic sports)
 Includes index.
 Summary: "Presents information about track and field in the
Olympics including events such as relays, hurdles, pole vault,
javelin throw, and shot put"– Provided by publisher.
ISBN 978-1-60753-810-3 (library binding)
ISBN 978-1-60753-899-8 (ebook)
ISBN 978-1-68152-051-3 (paperback)
1. Track and field–Juvenile literature. 2. Olympics–Juvenile
literature. I. Title.
 GV1060.55.D64 2016
 796.42–dc23
                                    2014045802

Editor: Wendy Dieker
Series Designer: Kathleen Petelinsek
Book Designer: Aubrey Harper
Photo Researcher: Derek Brown

Photo Credits: Harry How/Getty Images cover; Matt Slocum/
AP/Corbis 5; Chen Xiaowei/Xinhua Press/Corbis 6; Lucy
Nicholson/Reuters/Corbis 9; Lucy Nicholson/Reuters/Corbis
10; PCN/Corbis 13; Julian Finney/Getty Images 14-15; Kerim
Okten/epa/Corbis 17; Bernd Thissen/epa/Corbis 18; David
J. Phillip/AP/Corbis 20-21; Associated Press 22; Andy Rain/
epa/Corbis 25; Diego Azubel/epa/Corbis 26; Paul J Sutton/
PCN/Corbis 29

Printed in Malaysia

HC 10 9 8 7 6 5 4 3 2 1
PB 10 9 8 7 6 5 4 3 2 1

# Table of Contents

# Going for Gold

The crowd roars. The field is marked in chalk. Athletes from around the world line up to run, jump, and throw. It's track and field at the Olympic Games.

Track and field events have always been part of the games. From Ancient Greece to today, athletes have given their all as they go for the gold.

 Why is it called track and field?

And they are off! The men's 100-meter dash is one of the events at the Summer Olympics.

 The running events take place on a big oval track. Throwing and jumping events take place on a grassy field.

Gold medalist Usain Bolt from Jamaica sprints in the Olympic 200m in 2008.

# Running Events

On your marks! Get set! Go! Men and women **sprint** with blazing speed in short races. The shortest race is the 100–meter (100m) dash. This race lasts only about 10 seconds! Sprinters also run in the 200m and the 400m races. Every race is a burst of action. A hundredth of a second can mean a win or a loss.

**Relays** are all about teamwork. Each team has four runners. They take turns racing around the track. The first runner starts with a **baton**. He or she hands it off to the next runner. The last runner sprints to the finish line.

Relay races are two lengths. In the 4x100, each runner goes 100 meters. In the 4x400, each runner goes once around the track.

 How long is the Olympic track?

A US runner takes off after grabbing the baton from her teammate in the 4x400 relay.

 The track is 400 meters around.

**A Russian hurdler leaps over a hurdle in the 400m race at the 2012 Olympics.**

 How high is a hurdle in the men's 110m?

A **hurdles** race is a sprint with jumping. Runners speed down their lanes. As they run, they leap over the hurdles on the track. One missed jump can send a runner crashing down to the track! With such short races, a fall will cost the race. These sprints are a true test of speed and strength.

Hurdles stand 42 inches (1.07 m) high. Women's are shorter for the 100m race. They are 33 inches (0.84 m) high.

Long-distance running is about having energy for a long time. Runners need to pace themselves. If they run too fast, they will get tired. But they can't go too slow. They might not catch up. On the track, races are from 800 meters to 10,000 meters. The longest race is the marathon. It is 26.2 miles (42.2 km) long! The race takes hours to finish!

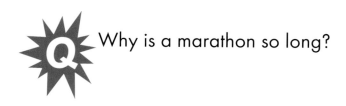 Why is a marathon so long?

**Runners bunch up on the track during the 5000m race. They will go 12.5 laps around the track.**

The race comes from an old Greek story about a soldier who ran about 26 miles (42 km) from Marathon to Athens.

# Jumping Events

Run! Jump! Long jumpers sprint down the **runway**. They jump into the air. Sand flies as they land in the pit. The longest jump wins.

Hop! Step! Jump! In the triple jump, athletes run and then string three jumps together. The total distance of the jumps is measured.

**Olympic long jumpers soar more than 23 feet (7m).**

High jumpers aren't after distance. Their goal is height. These athletes jump over a bar. The bar gets higher and higher with each jump. Each jumper's score is the highest bar they can jump over. How high can they jump? The best usually get higher than 6.5 feet (2 meters)!

 Why do high jumpers jump backwards?

**Swedish high jumper Emma Green does the Fosbury flop in the 2012 Olympics.**

High jumpers used to leap like hurdlers. In 1968, Dick Fosbury jumped headfirst. He easily won. Soon all high jumpers were doing the "Fosbury Flop."

A pole vaulter from Germany
uses a long pole to hurl
himself over a high bar.

 How high can pole vaulters soar?

Run. Plant. Fly! There's nothing like the pole vault. Vaulters use a long pole to soar to amazing heights. They start by running with a long pole toward a high bar. They plant the pole in a "box" at the end of the track. This launches them up to the bar. Vaulters arch their backs and soar over the bar. The highest vault wins!

 The Olympic record for men is 19.6 feet (5.97 meters). That means a pole vaulter could fly right over an adult giraffe!

# Throwing Events

How far can you throw a ball? Or a spear? Throwing events are all about strength and skill. In one event, athletes hurl a spear called a **javelin**. They run down a runway. Then they throw the spear as far as they can. The farthest throw wins.

Olympic javelin throws go nearly the length of a football field.

US athlete Trey Hardee
spins around before
throwing the flat discus.

Spin and then let it fly! Discus throwers hurl a heavy disc. First, they spin in a tight circle. Then they whip their arm around to throw the discus as far as they can.

The hammer throw is similar, but athletes throw a heavy ball on a long wire. Throwers grab the handle at the end of the wire. They spin around and around, faster and faster. Finally they let go. The hammer whizzes through the air. The longest throw wins.

Heave! The **shot put** event is about pure strength. Like other throwers, shot putters start by spinning around. Then they chuck the heavy, round shot as far as they can. It's not like throwing a baseball, though. A men's shot weighs just over 16 pounds (7.26 kg). That's almost 50 times heavier than a baseball!

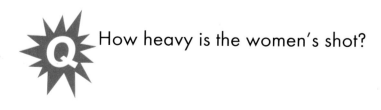 How heavy is the women's shot?

Shot putters tuck the shot under their chin while they get ready to launch it across the field.

 It weighs 8.8 pounds (4 kg).

US athlete Ashton Eaton won the 2012 Olympic decathlon.

# All-Around Events

The world's top all-around athletes can do it all. They run. They jump. They throw. Ancient Greek athletes competed in the pentathlon. It had five events. Today, the **decathlon** challenges men in ten events. They battle for the top spot in four runs, three jumps, and three throws. Some call the winner the world's greatest athlete.

What about the best women? These women compete in seven events called the **heptathlon**. They run three races, do two jumping events, and fire off two throws.

There's a lot going on in the stadium. You'll find speed. You'll see strength. Cheer on your country's top stars at the Summer Olympics.

**British athlete Jessica Ennis won the Olympic heptathlon in 2012.**

# Glossary

**baton** A short stick handed from one runner to another during a relay race.

**decathlon** The men's all-around track and field competition that includes ten events.

**heptathlon** The women's all-around track and field competition that includes seven events.

**hurdles** Small fences on the track for runners to jump over during a sprint race.

**javelin** A spear used in throwing events.

**relay** A race that a team of people do; each runner takes a turn running part of the race.

**runway** A strip of track where jumpers and javelin throwers run to gain speed.

**shot put** An event where an athlete throws a heavy steel ball as far as possible.

**sprint** To run as fast as possible for a short distance.

# Read More

**Frederick, Shane**. *Track & Field*. Mankato, Minn.: Creative Education, 2012.

**Hunter, Nick**. *The 2012 London Olympics*. Chicago: Heinemann, 2012.

**Peters, Stephanie True**. *Great Moments in the Summer Olympics*. New York: Little, Brown and Co., 2012.

# Websites

**Athletics | Olympic.org**
*www.olympic.org/athletics*

**Track and Field | NBC Olympics**
*http://nbcolympics.com/sport/track-and-field/*

**USA Track and Field**
*http://www.usatf.org/Sports/Track---Field.aspx*

# Index

# About the Author

Author and editor Matt Doeden has written hundreds of children's and young adult books. Some of his books have been listed among the Best Children's Books of the Year by the Children's Book Committee at Bank Street College. Doeden lives in Minnesota with his wife and two children.